YOUR KNOWLEDGE HAS VALUE

AF167119

Japanese tea ceremony. Philosophy of "wabi sabi"

GRIN ☺

Bibliographic information published by the German National Library:

The German National Library lists this publication in the National Bibliography; detailed bibliographic data are available on the Internet at http://dnb.dnb.de.

ISBN: 9783346662422
This book is also available as an ebook.

© GRIN Publishing GmbH
Trappentreustraße 1
80339 München

Print and binding: Books on Demand GmbH, Norderstedt, Germany
Printed on acid-free paper from responsible sources.

The present work has been carefully prepared. Nevertheless, authors and publishers do not incur liability for the correctness of information, notes, links and advice as well as any printing errors.

GRIN web shop: https://www.grin.com/document/1214491

SEMINARARBEIT

Rahmenthema des wissenschaftspropädeutischen Seminars:

Leitfach: Englisch

Thema der Arbeit: The Simple Beauty of Tea

Abgabetermin: *10.11.2020*

Table of Contents

1. Introduction

> Tea is nought but this:
> First you heat the water,
> Then you make the tea.
> Then you drink it properly.
> That is all you need to know.[1]

The previous lines are a poem composed by Sen no Rikyu (1522-1591) one of the greatest tea masters to conduct the simple and humble Japanese tea ceremony. To make tea one must boil the water, add the tea, and drink it properly. This is all there is to know, tea is not more and not less.

After tea is brought from China to Japan its spirit is first valued as a refined way to escape the world, subsequent its effect as a medicine is appreciated, and it soon develops into a lavish ceremony merely focusing on its pleasant taste. In all these forms tea serves the Japanese population, at first being accessible to the small wealthy aristocracy and priesthood before spreading over Japan, but in all these forms tea is either complicated, rational or extravagant, either forgetting its simplicity or missing an adequate gratitude to drink it properly. Thus, these lines prove of a shift in the perception of tea now appreciating its simplicity in a modest way. Nevertheless, to attain simplicity and a feeling for modesty one must walk a long path.[2]

2. A Short History of Tea

The Tea ceremony in Japan has a long history and undergoes various changes throughout the centuries. As Kakuzo Okakura states in "The Book of Tea" Japan as a country develops on its own, isolated from the continent, creating a unique culture based on tea[3] even though it is formed by the Chinese culture at the beginning. A.L. Sadler writes in his book "The Japanese Tea Ceremony" that the first tea-party in Japan is held in the first half of the 9th century.[4] In "Tea Life, Tea Mind", Soshitsu Sen relates the 12th century as the beginning of the spreading of Tea.[5] Both are correct. Sen Soshitsu

---

[1] Sen, Soshitsu XV: *Tea Life, Tea Mind*, John Weatherhill, Japan 1979, p.44.
[2] cf. Sen Soshitsu 1979, pp.44f.
[3] cf. Okakura, Kakuzo: *The Book of Tea*, 1st edition by Penguin Classics, UK 2016, p.4.
[4] cf. Sadler, Arthur Lindsay: *The Japanese Tea Ceremony, Cha-no-yu and the Zen Art of Mindfulness*, Tuttle Publishing, China 2019, pp.5f.
[5] cf. Sen Soshitsu 1979, p.11.

mentions in his record "The Japanese Way of Tea" the possibility of tea having existed in Japan even in 729 though there is no reliable evidence.[6] He further confirms that the first available records of tea-drinking date back to 814/815. During the Heian era (794-1192) Japanese students and monks are sent to China to study their traditions and bring back tea. Tea remains a rarity, though, and is primarily accessible to aristocrats and priests who, replacing wine with tea, drink it to escape the mundane world into a "world apart"[7] which is free. They view tea as poetic and seek refinement as well as a connection to advanced China by imitating the Chinese culture and using the extravagant Chinese utensils. Only little remains from their customs and tea falls partly into oblivion. Further, Japan becomes culturally more independent during the Kamakura era (1192-1333). Eisai (also Yosai, 1141-1215) travels to China in 1191 returning with new tea seeds and Zen Buddhism. In the following he writes the "Kissa Yojo Ki" ("Drinking Tea for Health")[8] thus reawakening the tradition of drinking tea, this occasion is mentioned in 'Tea Life, Tea Mind'. As Eisai convinces of the beverage's benefits for health it is appreciated among the upper classes. Zen monks also appreciate its effect to overcome sleepiness hence supporting their meditation, and soon develop tea-drinking into a ritual in Zen temples. In the transition from the Kamakura to the Muromachi era (1333-1573) the warrior class, the Samurai, emerges. Contrary to the wealthy in the Heian era they live in the insecurity of the Sengoku Jidai ("Age of Warring States" (1467-1568))[9]. The Warriors have a rational approach towards tea which makes an increasing production possible and tea becomes widely accessible. They appreciate the beverage for its pleasant taste but also hold lavish tea parties to demonstrate their power, hereby creating tea-tasting contests serving for entertainment.[10] To Soshitsu it appears the participants at these contests seek "in this glittering world of excess a means to escape from their uncertain times".[11]

At the end of the 15th century Murata Shuko (also Juko, 1422-1502) connects the spiritual and quotidian aspects of tea in his "Way of Tea" distinguishing it from the aspect of luxurious

---

[6] This date is also mentioned by Okakura 2016, p.27.
[7] Sen, Soshitsu XV: *The Japanese Way of Tea, From Its Origins in China to Sen Rikyu,* University of Hawai'i Press, USA 1998, p.122.
[8] Ibid. p.58.
[9] The Sengoku Jidai is a period of social upheaval and civil wars during the Muromachi era but the age of wars only becomes peaceful at the end of the Azuchi-Momoyama Period (1573-1603) after Oda Nobunaga and Toyotomi Hideyoshi succeed in uniting Japan. (Nakasendo Way and Walk Japan Ltd. (n.d.): *The Warring States Period.* https://www.nakasendoway.com/the-warring-states-period/ (last access: 06/11/2020) and The Editors of Encyclopaedia Britannica (1998): *Azuchi-Momoyama Period, Japan History.* https://www.britannica.com/event/Azuchi-Momoyama-period (last access: 06/11/2020)).
[10] cf. Sen Soshitsu 1998, pp.47-50, 57f, 75, 79, 89f, 119ff.
[11] Sen Soshitsu 1979, pp.11f.

entertainment.[12] Shuko starts drinking tea to avoid falling asleep in Zen class, and consumes it regularly thereafter.[13] As Sadler states Shuko also offers tea to his friends in a ceremonial way while they enjoy the Japanese poetry.[14] Shuko sees in the linked verse the spirit of tea as both aim for a "cold and withered" style. To him tea can purify one's heart and its ideal is in Zen.[15] Eventually combining tea with Zen[16] Shuko makes the ceremony simpler and humbler, introducing new rules to the tea ceremony which serve as the foundation for today's *chanoyu*[17].[18]

Shuko's ritual flourishes especially among merchants, who are often introduced to the Art of Zen.[19] Takeno Joo (also Sho'o, 1502-1555), born into a family of merchants, first studies poetry but is also introduced to Zen and tea as it is considered a fashion at the time.[20] Becoming the greatest tea master after Shuko he develops Shuko's teachings and is the first to refer to the "cold and withered" as wabi; thus, evolving tea to wabi cha[21].[22] Later he takes Sen no Rikyu as his disciple. Rikyu simplifies the ceremony so that anyone can conduct it. His accomplishments are the ones to completely evolve and establish the tea ceremony as well as a life based on tea. Often most achievements are ascribed to him, erroneously defining him as the only founder of the ceremony. Nevertheless, it is righteous to think of him as one of the greatest tea masters who elates tea to its maxim and whose teachings shape the spirit of the ceremony until today.[23] His ideals will be stated in the course of this paper.

As it is perceivable in the history of tea the tea-drinking tradition and the Way of Tea are closely related to Zen Buddhism as well as to Politics which both highly influence the arts.

---

[12] cf. Sen Soshitsu 1998, p.140.
[13] cf. ibid. p.127.
[14] cf. Sadler 2019, pp.105f.
[15] cf. Sen Soshitsu 1998, pp. 129, 131, 133.
[16] It is mentioned by Sen Soshitsu that Shuko acts according to his Zen teacher Ikkyu (1394-1481) (Sen Soshitsu 1998, p. 128) Andrew Juniper however names Ikkyu as the actual founder of the Way (Juniper, Andrew: *Wabi Sabi, The Japanese Art of Impermanence*, Tuttle Publishing, Singapore 2003, pp. 34ff).
[17] Meaning "hot water for tea", refers to the tea ceremony.
[18] cf. Sen Soshitsu 1979, p.12.
[19] cf. ibid. p.12.
[20] cf. Sadler 2019, pp.109f.
[21] *Cha* means *tea*.
[22] cf. Sen Soshitsu 1998, pp.146-148, 152.
[23] cf. Sen Soshitsu 1979, pp.12f, and Juniper, Andrew, *Wabi Sabi, The Japanese Art of Impermanence*, Tuttle Publishing, Singapore 2003, pp.40ff (this source can be viewed as an example glorifying Rikyu, nevertheless, in comparison to other sources its content is considered correct (cp. Plutschow, Herbert: *Rediscovering Rikyu and the Beginnings of the Japanese tea Ceremony*. Especially pp.112-142)).

2.1 Zen Buddhism

Zen Buddhism is an offspring of the Indian Buddhism which emerges in the 6th century BC after its founder Siddhartha Gautama Buddha (ca. 600-400 BC)[24] dies. China introduces Buddhism to Japan in the 6th century. Zen Buddhism is discovered by Eisai during his journey to China in 1191 where he hopes to find a Buddhist discipline to reawaken the Buddhist faith in Japan.[25]

Zen contains Buddhist elements, nonetheless it is close to Taoism, a Chinese philosophical religion which can be referred to as "the art of being in the world"[26], accepting the given circumstances of life. Like Taoism Zen does not like to be defined. Thus, answers on the question of Zen are vague and obscure.[27]

Zen signifies meditation,[28] and meditation is one of the main practices in Zen, at which the right posture (in general: sitting straight with one's legs crossed) reflects the right state of mind, which is called by Shunryu Suzuki the "beginner's mind"[29] referring to a pure, self-sufficient mind full of possibilities as it is not limited like the mind of one who believes to be wise. Self-sufficiency or sufficiency in general is of utter importance since Zen monks are non-materialistic and possess only the necessary.[30] Zen teaches the oneness of all things refusing the view of a dualistic world. The dualistic view of the world consists e.g. in the idea that non-singular things are plural. In dualism body and mind may be considered as one union or two separate unities, however they are neither one nor two, "body and mind are both two and one".[31] Furthermore, oneness means that everything is one, so one must be aware that another is oneself.[32] Whereas dualism implies that everything which is not part of oneself is separate thus causing egoism which, too, must be outpaced to attain a better understanding of the world.[33]In tea the aspect of Oneness consists in the harmony between

---

[24] Siddhartha Gautama is the first Buddha, and Buddhism is based on his teachings. He is born a prince but, affected by the suffering of those outside the palace, he decides to live in material poverty. Eventually finding a medium between overindulgence and self-denial to avoid suffering and to find unconditional and long lasting happiness which is also referred to as "the state of enlightenment, of Buddhahood" (Diamond Way Buddhism (2020): *The life of the Buddha.* https://www.diamondway-buddhism.org/buddhism/buddha/ (last access: 06.11.2020) and Juniper 2003, pp.15f). This state of mind can only be achieved through meditation.
[25] cf. Plutschow, Herbert: *Rediscovering Rikyu and the Beginnings of the Japanese Tea Ceremony*, GLOBAL ORIENTAL, Folkestone 2003, p.25.
[26] Juniper 2003, p.17.
[27] cf. Juniper 2003, pp.17f, 20, 22.
[28] cf. Okakura 2016, p.43.
[29] Shunryu, Suzuki: *Zen Mind, Beginner's Mind,* John Weatherhill, Japan 1975, p. 21.
[30] cf. Juniper 2003, p.22.
[31] Shunryu 1975, p.25.
[32] cf. Kapleau, Philip: *The Three Pillars of Zen, Teaching, Practice, and Enlightenment,* Anchor Books, USA 1980, pp.61f.
[33] cf. Juniper 2003, p.24.

host and guest and all the utensils used during the ceremony, striving for *muhinshu* (nondifferentiation) among them.[34]

Zen Buddhists, like Buddhists, aim for enlightenment to stop the cycle of rebirth and the suffering connected to it, they aim for *nirvana*[35]. For that daily practice is essential and the teachings must be embodied and transmitted to daily life. Such is a goal of The Way of Tea. Only with effort and practice the ceremony can be embodied becoming a natural part of one's existence.[36]

Death as well is non-dualistic. Dying is not equal to the end of life nor is life eternal nor does the body cease to exist while the mind does not. It is a state of existing and not existing.[37] Nevertheless, death is assured and life short, hence it is important to live and appreciate each moment.[38] This philosophy is represented in *"ichigo ichie"* (one time, one meeting)[39] which as well plays a major role in tea turning each gathering into a unique experience.[40]

Since Rikyu's time tea serves as a way of self-discovery aiming for enlightenment. It is considered that "Tea and the Way of Buddha are the same".[41]

2.2 Tea and Politics

As a ritual tea can be transformatory or confirmatory. The former aims to transform society, especially during war it tends to transmit peace and equality, putting aside hierarchy whereas the latter longs for confirmation of the already existing, meaning that it supports hierarchy in peaceful times and helps people accept the governing system.[42]

---

[34] cf. Sen Soshitsu 1979, p.40.

[35] Nirvana and Enlightenment are sometimes used synonymously though their understanding can vary depending on the Buddhist teaching. Enlightenment is often referred to as "awakening", realizing the true nature and emptiness of all things as well as the non-existence of dualism in the world, whereas Nirvana can be translated as "liberation" and is a "state of being beyond existence and non-existence" only an awakened one can achieve. It also refers to death. Shunryu Suzuki explains that "to attain Nirvana is to pass away" or better "to pass on". (Shunryu 1975, p.93 and O'Brien, Barbara (27.02.2019): *Enlightenment and Nirvana, Can you have one without the other?* https://www.learnreligions.com/enlightenment-and-nirvana-449967 (last access: 06/11/2020) and Bhikshu, Kusala (n.d.): *Buddhist Enlightenment vs Nirvana.* http://www.urbandharma.org/udharma6/enlightnirvana.html (last access: 06.11.2020)).

[36] cf. Sen Soshitsu 1979, p.50.

[37] Bhikshu, Kusala (n.d.): *Buddhist Enlightenment vs Nirvana.* http://www.urbandharma.org/udharma6/enlightnirvana.html (last access: 06/11/2020).

[38] cf. Shunryu 1975, pp. 21f, 25f, 37.

[39] This phrase is often used by Joo to emphasize that no event can be duplicated in his case especially referring to tea gatherings and to the importance of concentrating on the ceremony instead of on mundane concerns. (Sen Soshitsu 1998, p.156).

[40] cf. Sen Soshitsu 1979, p.41.

[41] *Chado Koten Zenshu,* vol.10, 1956, p.279 according to Plutschow 2003, p.31.

[42] cf. Plutschow 2003, p.19.

As an art tea needs political support to exist and develop, therefore it is controlled by the political leaders and not entirely free to evolve on its own.[43] A shift in the meaning of tea is especially noticeable when comparing the Heian era, whose leaders aim for the recreation of the Chinese culture, and the Muromachi era with the Warrior's completely different approach to tea.[44] With the emerging of the warrior class tea is increasingly integrated into politics.[45]

Under the leadership of Oda Nobunaga (1534-1582) and Toyotomi Hideyoshi (1536-1598), who aim to unify Japan, *wabi cha* serves as a means to celebrate victories as well as to talk to the enemy, since the tearoom is a neutral ground in which both parties feel safe. Also, tea utensils, being expensive and of high value, represent the power of the host and are often gifted as a sign of respect and the willingness to cooperate. Hence the nation could be controlled from inside a tearoom.[46]

3. Wabi Sabi

There are diverse attempts in translating this term. *Wabi* may be translated as "solitude".[47] One may also analyse its verb form *wabu* meaning "to languish" or as an adjective *wabishii*, the "sense of loneliness". Whereas *sabi* may be seen as the "sense of desolation".[48] Kakuzo Okakura specifies *wabi sabi* as "a worship of the imperfect"[49]. However, like Zen the true essence of *wabi sabi* can hardly be grasped with words but must be experienced. According to the Zen belief words are the cause for misunderstanding, therefore Zen monks use the Art of wabi sabi to express their ideals, to express the truths of the world.[50]

Humility, sincerity, asymmetry, imperfection, and impermanence. These are connected to *wabi sabi*. It is a beauty which is in the detail and, showing its age and decay, reminds of the evanescence of life, creating a melancholic feeling. *Wabi sabi* as well is non-dualistic, not differentiating between ugliness and beauty, whereas dualism would interpret it as viewing the ugly as beautiful, though those are no contrasts. It seeks for creativity of the artist and the beholder, as it often remains unfinished so it can be completed in one's mind, so the true art is to be found in the room of

---

[43] cf. Plutschow 2003, p.42.
[44] cf. Sen Soshitsu 1998, p.119.
[45] cf. Plutschow 2003, pp.38, 42.
[46] cf. ibid. pp.44, 57, 80, 82-87, 90f.
[47] Oxford Lexico (n.d.). https://www.lexico.com/en/definition/wabi (last access: 06.11.2020).
[48] Juniper 2003, pp.48f.
[49] Okakura 2016, p.3.
[50] cf. Juniper 2003, pp. IX, 27.

9

imagination, in the space which can hold much more than the filled. The art further proves of a deep respect towards nature and life as the artist cares for each detail and lets nature express its own. Its simplicity remains in the focus on function, in its rusticity and imperfection. [51] *Wabi sabi* is "profound artlessness and purity"[52] which most can feel but not explain.

Shuko's *wabi* is the "cold and withered" but can also be perceived in his saying that 'It is best to have a magnificent steed in a straw hut'[53] in which he describes the spirit of his *chanoyu*. Shuko refers to the usage of rare and valued tea utensils, which represent luxury, inside a simple and rough hut indicating poverty. This contrast supposes an emerging of *wabi* as a contrast to the popular tea contests, but also emphasises the tea utensils used[54] suggesting "richness beyond appearances".[55] Even closer to *wabi sabi* is Shuko's statement not to appreciate a cloudless moon as much as a partially hidden one as it is impermanent due to the moving clouds while allowing the mind to complete the image.[56]

Image 1: Black Raku Tea Bowl made by Chojiro (1516-?1592) during Momoyama period. Ceramic. Height, 9.2cm; Diameter, 9.5cm.

Rikyu's wabi sabi is perceivable in his preference for black Raku Tea Bowls (Image 1)[57]. Raku Bowls are made by the Raku family, principally by Chojiro. The bowls in general are simple and the shape is imperfect, Rikyu however preferred the black ones since they are "old heart"[58] thus incorporating *wabi sabi*.[59]

As *wabi sabi* is the aesthetic of Zen it highly influences the tea ceremony.

[51] cf. Juniper 2003, pp. 1f, 12, 87, 110f, 153, and Okakura 2016, pp. 42, 52.
[52] Juniper 2003, p.99.
[53] Yamanoe Soji, *Yamanoe Soji Ki*, in CKZ [*Chado Koten Zenshu*], vol.6, p.101 according to Sen Soshitsu 1998, p.141 and *Yamanoue Soji Ki*, in *Chado Koten Zenshu*, vol.6, 1956, p.101 according to Plutschow 2003, p.35 (variation of quote 'A precious horse tied to a shabby hut').
[54] cf. Sen Soshitsu 1998, p.141.
[55] Plutschow 2003, p.35.
[56] cf. ibid. p.36.
[57] cf. The Met 150 (n.d.): *Black Raku Tea Bowl, early 17th century*.
https://www.metmuseum.org/art/collection/search/62898 (last access: 06/11/2020).
[58] Plutschow 2003, p.102.
[59] cf. The Met 150 (n.d.): *Black Raku Tea Bowl, early 17th century*.
https://www.metmuseum.org/art/collection/search/62898 (last access: 06/11/2020) and Plutschow 2003, p.102.

4. The Influence of Tea

With the tea ceremony being the embodiment of Zen and *wabi sabi* it is philosophy, art, and religion. Various of its aspects are reflected in Japan's culture. Such is the physical and cultural Oneness of the Japanese people, their appreciation of the imperfect as well as the vague which leaves room for the own interpretation. It is perceivable in the Japanese modesty and their respectful attitude.[60] In Architecture the influence of tea becomes visible.

4.1 The Influence of Tea on Japan's Architecture

When arriving for a tea ceremony the guest first enters a simple gate before walking to the waiting area, waiting for the host to finish preparations the guest appreciates the garden.[61]

4.1.1 The Garden

With its moss-covered ground, the trees and shrubs, the tea garden resembles a forest, thus creating a tranquil space for *chanoyu*. The tea-master may further utilize rocks and streams referring to mountains and rivers to turn the small garden into an own world. The fence surrounding the garden symbolises the margin between the spiritual world of tea and the mundane. To leave the material world of concerns the guest walks the *roji*, the "dewy path" (Image 2)[62] . Consisting of irregular stepping-stones, the path, reminding of a mountain trail, guides to the tea hut, leading through the thoroughly but naturally arranged garden which reflects the season and the time of the day. E.g. the garden may be carefully swept but in autumn the leaves will cover the ground in memory of the vanishing life. The tea hut itself is built of natural and simple materials, like wood and bamboo, thus seeming to merge with the nature surrounding it. Nevertheless, the simplicity and appearing poverty misleads as solely materials of high quality and artistry are used and garden, roji and hut are expensive.[63]

This figure has been removed by GRIN for copyright reasons.

Image 2: Roji
Located in the main Hall of Kennin-ji Zen Temple in Kyoto

---

[60] cf. Juniper 2003, p. 53-57.
[61] cf. Sen Soshitsu 1979, p.27 and Plutschow 2003, p.11.
[62] cf. Bourne Mark (13/01/2015): *Seeing the Japanese Garden*. https://www.japanesegardening.org/site/seeing-the-japanese-garden/ (last access: 07/11/2020).
[63] cf. Juniper 2003, pp.69-74 and Plutschow 2003, pp.55f and Sen Soshitsu 1979, pp.27, 45 and Okakura 2016, pp.53f, 57.

4.1.2 The Tea Hut

Kakuzo Okakura defines the tea ceremony as "a religion of aestheticism"[64] with the tearoom as its temple.[65] Initially tearooms were wide luxurious rooms to hold tea contests. Shuko is the first to secede from large rooms of prestige to small ones. His smallest room is a four-and-a-half tatami-mat room (a tatami mat is about 182cm x 91cm). Thereafter the tearooms tend to become smaller, the smallest tearoom, designed by Rikyu, is a one-and-a-half mats room. The size reflects the "non-existence of space to the truly enlightened"[66] and further implies intimacy. Rikyu as well claims that the smaller the room the more people find space within it, however only a true master can conduct *chanoyu* in such a little room.[67]

The entrance, too, diminishes in size. First being high enough for a man to enter in straight position Rikyu soon introduces the *Nijiriguchi*, a crawling-in door, having a height less than one meter even the tiniest person has to bow

This figure has been removed by GRIN for copyright reasons.

Image 3: Tea House

to enter the room; thus also showing his respect. No difference is made between a wealthy lord and a poor merchant, everyone bows, and everyone is equal. A warrior must leave his weapons outside, as a sword will not pass the door, also symbolising the aspect of peace inside the hut. The room's windows are normally covered with bamboo and paper to control the light inside (Rikyu e.g. likes dark tearooms). In the alcove a scroll or flower suggesting the theme of the gathering is placed. Beside the alcove is the hearth to heat the water for tea and the utensils needed for preparation. The *katte-guchi* at the back is the host's entrance, so he can go in and out without disturbing the guests. In the anteroom the utensils are washed and stored.[68] (Image 3)[69]

---

[64] Okakura 2016, p.3.
[65] cf. Juniper 2003, p.31.
[66] Okakura 2016, p.56.
[67] cf. Plutschow 2003, p.122 and Sen Soshitsu 1998, p.139.
[68] cf. Sen Soshitsu 1998, pp.167f and Okakura 2016, pp.53, 56, 58 and Plutschow 2003, p.102 and Sadler 2019, pp.17, 29 and Matsuyama, Hiroko (25.07.2017): *Japanese Tea House: Architecture of Ultimate Spiritual World.* https://www.patternz.jp/japanese-tea-house-architecture/ (last access: 07.11.2020).
[69] cf. Matsuyama, Hiroko (25.07.2017): *Japanese Tea House: Architecture of Ultimate Spiritual World.* https://www.patternz.jp/japanese-tea-house-architecture/ (last access: 07.11.2020).

5. The Japanese Tea

5.1 Chanoyu

The tea ceremony consists of small steps of philosophical, religious, and ritual importance. Furthermore, the ceremonies can vary depending on the master conducting it. Due to its complexity and variety merely a general structure will be roughly stated.

The ceremony already commences with its preparations. The host has to invite the guests, clean and arrange the tearoom, the garden path and the tea utensils. In the alcove a scroll suggesting the theme for the gathering or a flower may be placed, the hearth is lit with fresh charcoal and the kettle with water for tea is placed upon in.

The guests arrive before the appointed hour, the open gate welcoming them. The host silently invites the guests inside before they proceed to the waiting area where they receive a cup of hot water. Once the master is ready, the guests follow the *roji* leading to the tea hut. At a stone basin next to the entrance the guests clean their hands and mouth, symbolically purifying themselves. Now they can enter the tea hut by crawling through the Nijiriguchi. Inside the house the guests are expected to inspect and appreciate the arrangement and all utensils displayed. Those utensils speak in the host's absence, therefore they must be carefully chosen to create the right atmosphere according to the suggested theme of the gathering.[70] Thereafter the guests sit down waiting for the host.

The host appears and welcomes the guests thanking for their presence before serving a light meal, the *kaiseki*[71]. Afterwards the guests go in the garden in order to appreciate nature and to refresh themselves while the host finishes preparations for serving tea. When ready he calls the guests back in. First thick tea is passed down in a bowl and the guests drink it according to a predefined order.[72] Until the finishing of thick tea barely any words are exchanged and in the silence the feeling of oneness is evoked.

---

[70] cf. Plutschow 2003, p.59.

[71] The name *kaiseki* originates from the warmed stones which are pressed against the stomach to relieve the feeling of hunger and cold. A technique primarily used by Zen monks though this lifestyle represents insufficiency and self-denial instead of the necessarily needed. The kaiseki is a small and simple seasonal meal to satisfy hunger. (Sen Soshitsu 1979, p.28).

[72] The firm order might seem to resemble a hierarchy, however, the main guest is not necessarily the wealthiest or most powerful.

In the following the guests closely examine the utensils e.g. asking about their name and origin. The utensils are then removed, and the host prepares thin tea at which each guest receives an own bowl of tea. The mood is now lighter, the guests may have short conversations and seek information about the displayed utensils.

The ceremony reaches its end. The guests eventually silent again, admire the flowers one last time and leave. The host stays at the entrance until every guest is out of sight. He then reflects upon the gathering for a while before cleaning the utensils and the room, leaving it empty. For both host and guests, this gathering is a unique moment that will never occur the same way again.[73]

5.2 The Way of Tea

The Way of Tea, also called *chado*, contains the spirit of *chanoyu*, but its practice is not solely for the tea ceremony, it is to be expanded into all of one's existence.[74] Soshitsu describes the Way of Tea as "the simple act of serving tea and receiving it with gratitude".[75] Thankfulness is fundamental for everything done in the daily life, and so is for tea.[76] This gratitude enables a person to find satisfaction and appreciation by simply drinking tea, which is an aim of chado.[77]

Thankfulness is also included in *kokoro ire*[78], an essential concept of the Way. It requires of the host entire dedication in the preparations for *chanoyu* for the guest's sake whereas the guest is expected to be accepting and to appreciate the host's devotion.[79]

5.2.1 Wa, Kei, Sei, Jaku – The Four Basic Principles

According to Rikyu harmony, respect, purity, and tranquillity form the spirit of *chado*. They are four principles which are practical rules as well as the tea's highest ideals.

The first element is harmony (*Wa*). Harmony represents the oneness between the people, the utensils used, the food served, and nature. In harmony host and guests become one and transcend their individual roles. The utensils harmonize with each other and with the suggested theme of the tea gathering. The food is seasonal reminding of nature and the weather which influence the

---

[73] Sen Soshitsu 1979, p.28f, and Plutschow 2003, pp.11ff.
[74] cf. ibid. p.11.
[75] Sen Soshitsu 1979, p.9.
[76] cf. ibid. p.17.
[77] cf. Zen Wonders (n.d.): *4 Principles Of Chado.* https://zenwondersmatcha.com.au/pages/4-principles-of-chado (last access: 06/11/2020).
[78] *Kokoro* means 'heart-spirit-mind', *ire* represents 'to put in'.
[79] cf. Sen Soshitsu 1779, pp.40f.

ceremony. Through harmony with nature one can understand "the evanescence of all things and the unchanging in the changing".[80]

Respect (*Kei*) consists in the equality inside the tearoom, in understanding and accepting the other even in disagreement and being considerate of him. Respect extends even towards objects and treating them carefully, not evaluating them by price or looks, thus appreciating the human investment in its creation as well as its origin, nature, is essential.

It is important for the garden path (*roji*), the tea house, and the tea utensils to be of natural cleanness. This cleanness represents purity (*Sei*) and refers to "clearing the 'dust of the world'"[81] implying to the freedom from the material. The act of cleaning allows the host to prepare for the tea ceremony and to create order in his spirit leading to a pure heart, solely with a pure and open heart one can accomplish harmony and respect.

The principle of tranquillity (*Jaku*) is a result. It is approached by one following the three principles of *Wa*, *Kei*, and *Sei*. *Jaku* is a state of selflessness and freedom similar to Enlightenment. The tranquil mind strengthens the significance of the tea gathering, and in company with others the tranquillity is deepened.[82]

5.2.2 The Seven Rules

Wa, Kei, Sei and Jaku are essential for the spirit of the tea ceremony, however they cannot be viewed as a guide. In response to the question what the most relevant aspects of a successful tea gathering are, Rikyu answers:

> Make a delicious bowl of tea ; lay the charcoal so that it heats the water ; arrange the flowers as they are in the field ; in summer suggest coolness, in winter warmth ; do everything ahead of time ; prepare for rain ; and give those with whom you find yourself every consideration.[83]

---

[80] Sen Soshitsu 1979, p.13.
[81] Sen Soshitsu 1979, p.14 (primary source not given).
[82] cf. ibid. p.13f, and The Urasenke Foundation, San Francisco (n.d.): *wa kei sei jaku*.
https://urasenke.org/characters/index.html (last access: 06/11/2020), and chanoyu.com, San Francisco, California (n.d.): *Wa Kei Sei Jaku*.
http://www.chanoyu.com/WaKeiSeiJaku.html#:~:text=Wa%20Kei%20Sei%20Jaku%20(harmony,integrate%20into%20t
heir%20daily%20lives. (last access: 06/11/2020), and Zen Wonders (n.d.): *4 Principles Of Chado*.
https://zenwondersmatcha.com.au/pages/4-principles-of-chado (last access: 06/11/2020).
[83] Sen Soshitsu 1979, p.31.

The student, unable to find any difficulty, is dissatisfied with the simplicity of those rules. Rikyu in the contrary suggests becoming the student's disciple if he was able to host a tea ceremony sticking to every norm. In the following each of the seven rules will be briefly explained.

"Make a delicious bowl of tea" refers to simply preparing a tasty bowl of tea. In any case Deliciousness is not based on the expense on tea and food, truly important is the sincere heart of the host. This sincerity includes an honest and complete dedication to the preparation of tea, free from the preoccupation to fail.

To *"lay the charcoal so that it heats the water"* must be learned. Solely an adequately arranged fire heats the water to the temperature necessary to bring out the tea's flavour. This rule indeed relies on the host's technical skill, but his knowledge should be used merely to please the guest.

Flowers represent beauty, arranging them correctly is considered an art.[84] One has to *"arrange the flowers as they are in the field"*, let them appear natural, which does not mean to place a number of flowers at random. The host may choose one single flower, which he treats with care and thoughtfulness, trying to express the whole life of that flower and enabling the guest to experience the beauty of all flowers in one.

"In summer suggest coolness, in winter warmth". Coolness and warmth in this case are not directly referred to the physical temperature and should not be mechanically produced. It is rather a suggestion to one's mind, by preparing the ceremony properly and thus creating a modest temperature for the body. E.g. the gathering might be set early in the morning in a dewy atmosphere, the roji might be sprinkled with water and the scroll hanging in the alcove proposes 'the one taste of coolness'.[85]

The fifth rule indicates the value of time. Rikyu advises the host to *"do everything ahead of time"*, thus respecting the time of oneself and of others. Therefore, the gathering must be minutely planned and errors and the unexpected must be considered.

"Prepare for rain" not only refers to the importance of umbrellas, it points at the ability to adapt to the unexpected with self-confidence and to correspond with circumstances "with an open heart and free and direct mind".[86]

---

[84] The flowers arrangement is called *chabana*. *Cha* means *tea*, *bana* derives from *hana* meaning *flower*. (chanoyu.com, San Francisco, California (n.d.): *Chabana*. http://www.chanoyu.com/WhatisChabana.html (last access: 06/11/2020)).
[85] Sen Soshitsu 1979, p.36.
[86] Sen Soshitsu 1979, p.38.

In a tea gathering the presence of host and guest is essential, and it is the interaction between them which makes them human.[87] *"Give those with whom you find yourself every consideration"* states a mutual regard between host and guest, allowing them to appreciate their moment together. Further creating a harmonious atmosphere in which host and guest become one.[88]

6. Conclusion

Tea in Japan takes on many forms as time passes. It can transform according to people's necessities serving as a means to escape the mundane, improve health, help to concentrate and entertain in tea contests. Initially solely accessible to a few, it soon spreads dominating the whole country, developing into an art of simplicity, beauty, and purity. As *chanoyu* is deeply rooted in Zen its philosophies appear complex and it requires effort to attain a complete understanding. Nevertheless maintaining an open and sincere heart allowing the ceremony to become part of you, the spirit of respect, harmony, purity and tranquillity will lead like a path to the true beauty of the world, consisting in the impermanence of life. This is the simple beauty of tea.

---

[87] The Japanese word for human is *ningen*. The word itself precisely explains its meaning, *nin* being the person and *gen* interval, hence being human consists of the interaction with others, (cf. Sen Soshitsu 1979, p.40).
[88] cf. Sen Soshitsu 1979, pp.31-40.

7. Glossary

Cha – Tea.

Chabana – art for flower arrangement; *cha* stands for tea and *bana* as a derivation of *hana*, the flower.

Chado – The Way of Tea.

Chanoyu – "hot water for tea", refers to the tea ceremony.

Ichigo Ichie – One time, one meeting.

Jaku – Tranquillity.

Katte-guchi – host's access to tea hut

Kei – Respect.

Kokoro Ire – *kokoro* means heart-spirit-mind, *Ire* to put in; requires dedication of the host and acceptance of the guest.

Muhinshu – *Mu* is nothingness, *hin* refers to the guest at the tea ceremony or to a disciple of Zen, *shu* is the host. *Muhinshu* is the nondifferentiation between host and guest.

Ningen – human; *nin* is person, *gen* represents interval.

Nijiriguchi – crawling door; entrance of the tea house less than one meter of height.

Nirvana – Blowing out, liberation, *death.*

Roji – dewy path; path leading to tea house

Sei – Purity.

Tatami mat – mat originally made of rice straw; about 182x91cm.

Wa – Harmony.

Wabi Sabi – *no direct translation* – The Art of Imperfection and Impermanence.

Zen – derives from the Word Dhayana meaning meditation.

8. Bibliography

8.1 Images

Image 1: The Met 150 (n.d.): *Black Raku Tea Bowl, early 17th century.*
https://www.metmuseum.org/art/collection/search/62898 (last access: 06/11/2020)

Image 2: Bourne Mark (13/01/2015): *Seeing the Japanese Garden.*
https://www.japanesegardening.org/site/seeing-the-japanese-garden/ (last access: 07/11/2020)

Image 3: Matsuyama, Hiroko (25/07/2017): *Japanese Tea House: Architecture of Ultimate Spiritual World.* https://www.patternz.jp/japanese-tea-house-architecture/ (last access: 07/11/2020)

8.2 Printed sources

Juniper, Andrew: *Wabi Sabi, The Japanese Art of Impermanence,* Tuttle Publishing, Singapore 2003

Kapleau, Philip: *The Three Pillars of Zen, Teaching, Practice, and Enlightenment,* Anchor Books, USA 1980

Sadler, Arthur Lindsay: *The Japanese Tea Ceremony, Cha-no-yu and the Zen Art of Mindfulness,* Tuttle Publishing, China 2019

Sen, Soshitsu XV: *Tea Life, Tea Mind*, John Weatherhill, Japan 1979

Sen, Soshitsu XV: *The Japanese Way of Tea, From Its Origins in China to Sen Rikyu,* University of Hawai'i Press, USA 1998

Shunryu, Suzuki: *Zen Mind, Beginner's Mind,* John Weatherhill, Japan 1975

Okakura, Kakuzo: *The Book of Tea*, 1st edition by Penguin Classics, UK 2016

Plutschow, Herbert: *Rediscovering Rikyu and the Beginnings of the Japanese Tea Ceremony*, GLOBAL ORIENTAL, Folkestone 2003

8.3 Internet sources

Bhikshu, Kusala (n.d.): *Buddhist Enlightenment vs Nirvana.*
http://www.urbandharma.org/udharma6/enlightnirvana.html (last access: 06/11/2020)

chanoyu.com, San Francisco, California (n.d.): *Chabana.*
http://www.chanoyu.com/WhatisChabana.html (last access: 06/11/2020)

chanoyu.com, San Francisco, California (n.d.): *Wa Kei Sei Jaku.*
http://www.chanoyu.com/WaKeiSeiJaku.html#:~:text=Wa%20Kei%20Sei%20Jaku%20(harmony,int
egrate%20into%20their%20daily%20lives. (last access: 06/11/2020)

Diamond Way Buddhism (n.d.), *The life of the Buddha.*
https://www.diamondway-buddhism.org/buddhism/buddha/ (last access: 06/11/2020)

Matsuyama, Hiroko (25.07.2017): *Japanese Tea House: Architecture of Ultimate Spiritual World.*
https://www.patternz.jp/japanese-tea-house-architecture/ (last access: 07/11/2020)

Nakasendo Way and Walk Japan Ltd. (n.d.): *The Warring States Period.*
https://www.nakasendoway.com/the-warring-states-period/ (last access: 06/11/2020)

O'Brien, Barbara (27.02.2019): *Enlightenment and Nirvana, Can you have one without the other?*
https://www.learnreligions.com/enlightenment-and-nirvana-449967 (last access: 06/11/2020)

Oxford Lexico (n.d.): *wabi..* https://www.lexico.com/en/definition/wabi (last access: 06/11/2020)

The Editors of Encyclopaedia Britannica (20.07.1998): *Azuchi-Momoyama Period, Japan History.*
https://www.britannica.com/event/Azuchi-Momoyama-period (last access: 06/11/2020)

The Met 150 (n.d.): *Black Raku Tea Bowl, early 17th century.*
https://www.metmuseum.org/art/collection/search/62898 (last access: 06/11/2020)

The Urasenke Foundation San Francisco (n.d.): *wa kei sei jaku.*
https://urasenke.org/characters/index.html (last access: 06/11/2020)

Zen Wonders (n.d.): *4 Principles Of Chado.*
https://zenwondersmatcha.com.au/pages/4-principles-of-chado (last access: 06/11/2020)